READING/WRITING COMPANION

Mc
Graw
Hill
Education

Cover: Nathan Love, Erwin Madrid

mheducation.com/prek-12

Copyright © McGraw-Hill Education

Send all inquiries to:
McGraw-Hill Education
Two Penn Plaza
New York, NY 10121

ISBN: 978-0-07-901811-3
MHID: 0-07-901811-4

Printed in the United States of America.

5 6 7 8 9 LMN 23 22 21 20   B

Welcome to Wonders!

Read exciting **Literature**, **Science**, and **Social Studies** texts!

★ **LEARN** about the world around you!

★ **THINK**, **SPEAK**, and **WRITE** about genres!

★ **COLLABORATE** in discussion and inquiry!

★ **EXPRESS** yourself!

my.mheducation.com

Use your student login to read core texts, practice grammar and spelling, explore research projects and more!

GENRE STUDY 1 NARRATIVE NONFICTION

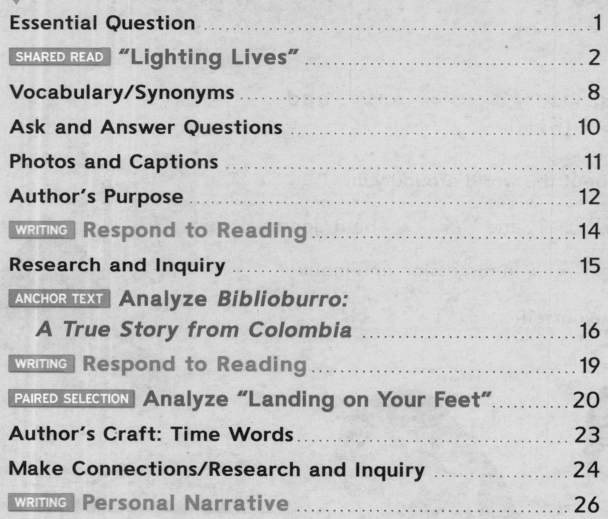

 Digital Tools Find this eBook and other resources at **my.mheducation.com**

Alison Wright/Corbis

GENRE STUDY 2 FICTION

GENRE STUDY 3 EXPOSITORY TEXT

WRAP UP THE UNIT

jianying yin/Getty Images

Talk About It

This garden was once an empty lot filled with garbage. Neighbors thought of a solution to this problem. They cleaned up the lot and planted a garden.

Talk with a partner about what is happening in the picture. What are some ways you can help out in your community? Write your ideas on the web.

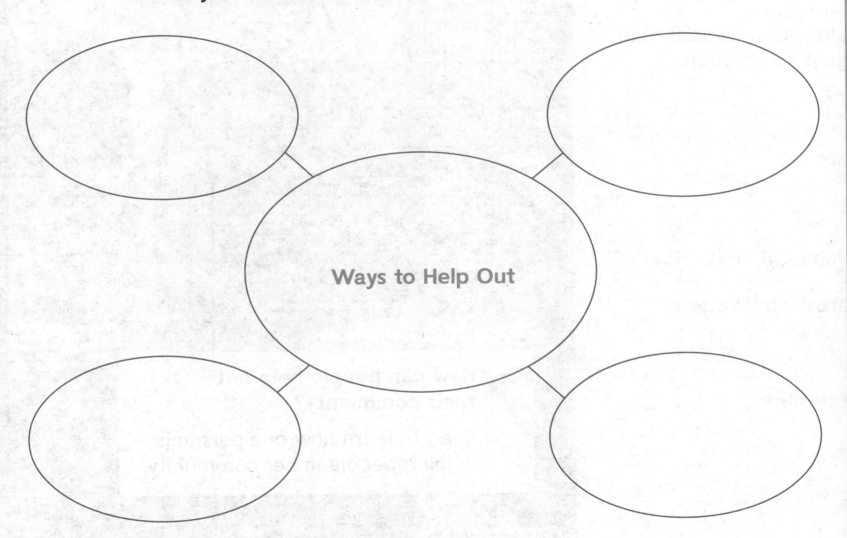

Ways to Help Out

TAKE NOTES

Asking questions helps you figure out what information you want to learn.

Write your questions here to gain information.

_____

_____

_____

As you read, make note of:

Interesting Words: _____

_____

Key Details: _____

_____

_____

_____

Lighting Lives

Essential Question

? How can people help out their community?

Read to learn how one person is helping people in her community.

When Debby Tewa was your age, her home had no electricity. She could not flip a light switch to read at night. She lit a candle. She could not cook on a stove or in a microwave oven. Her family cooked over a fire.

Debby lived in Arizona. When she was ten, she moved to a new home. Her new home had electricity! She could turn on a lamp and use a phone. She liked it!

Debby Tewa lived in a home that had small windows like this one. There was not a lot of light.

FIND TEXT EVIDENCE

Read

Paragraph 1

Author's Purpose

Underline what the author explains about Debby's home at your age. **Circle** how she read at night and how her family cooked.

Paragraph 2

Combine Information

How did Debby's life change when she was ten?

_____

_____

_____

Reread

Author's Craft

How does the author help you understand what Debby's home was like when she was your age?

FIND TEXT EVIDENCE

Read

Paragraph 1

Author's Purpose

Underline details that explain the way people use solar panels.

Paragraph 2

Ask and Answer Questions

Ask a question about where Debby went to work. Write it below.

_____

_____

_____

Circle text evidence that helps you to answer it.

Reread

Author's Craft

How does the author use punctuation to show when Debby was excited?

As she grew, Debby realized she wanted to learn more about solar power. Solar power is electricity that comes from the Sun. Solar panels are put on the roof of a building. The sunlight hits these panels and turns into electricity.

Debby thought a lot about solar power. Then she had an **idea**! She was excited. She went to work for a company that provided solar power to people's homes. She believed it would be a good **solution** for people who had no electricity. Debby likes solving problems!

Solar panels are now used on many homes.

Debby also thought of people in **villages** like the one she lived in as a child. The people in these small towns did not have any electricity. Solar power would work well there because there is a lot of sun in Arizona. Debby decided to help these families get solar power.

To get a family started, Debby helps them **borrow** money from a bank to buy the panels. After they get the money from the bank, they have some time to pay the money back. And the good news is there is no cost for using the sun's power!

(c) Ellen McKnight/Alamy

FIND TEXT EVIDENCE

Read

Paragraph 1
Synonyms
Circle a word with almost the same meaning as *villages*. What did Debby decide to do for families in places without electricity?

_____

_____

_____

Author's Purpose
Underline the sentence that explains how Debby helps a family buy panels.

Reread
Author's Craft

How does the author help you understand why solar energy is a good solution for people Debby helps?

Read

Paragraph 1
Photos and Captions

Draw a box around information that tells about the photograph.

What does Debby do when she travels to the countryside?

_____

_____

Paragraph 2
Ask and Answer Questions

Underline text evidence that answers the question: How does Debby help Hopi children?

Debby travels **across** lands outside cities in Arizona and New Mexico. She travels to the **countryside**. She helps Hopi and Navajo people get solar power.

Debby believes deeply in her work and **insists** that families learn about how solar power can help them. They are happy to do what she demands. Debby also travels to schools and summer camps to teach Hopi children about solar energy.

Debby helps many Hopi people.

bkgd) Luc Novovitch/Alamy; (I) Alison Wright/Corbis

Debby drives her truck from place to place. It is **lonely** with no one riding along. Then she thinks about how exciting it was to use electricity for the first time. Now families can do the things you do without thinking about them. They can heat their homes or turn on a light! Debby says she is "lighting up people's lives."

Summarize

Use the most important details from "Lighting Lives" to orally summarize how Debby Tewa helps her community get electricity.

NARRATIVE NONFICTION

FIND TEXT EVIDENCE

Read

Author's Purpose
Circle the description of what it is like when Debby drives from place to place. **Underline** what Debby thinks about.

Fluency

With a partner, read aloud page 7. Use the author's ideas and end punctuation to guide your expression.

Reread
Author's Craft

What does Debby mean when she says she is "lighting up people's lives"? Why does the author include this quote?

Vocabulary

Use the sentences to talk with a partner about each word. Then answer the questions.

across
We walked **across** the street.

What are other things you can walk across?

_____

_____

borrow
I like to **borrow** books from the library.

What can you borrow from a friend?

_____

_____

> ✎ **Build Your Word List** Choose a word that you noted while reading. Use a print or digital thesaurus to look up synonyms for the word. Use one pair of synonyms in your own sentences.

countryside
The **countryside** is full of grass and trees.

What else may be in the countryside?

_____

_____

idea
Kate has an **idea** for the class project.

Name an idea you have for a game to play.

_____

_____

insists
Mom **insists** we wear our seatbelts.

What is something your teacher insists that you and your classmates do?

_____

_____

_____

lonely

The boy was **lonely** when his friend moved away.

When have you felt lonely?

_____

_____

solution

Dylan found a **solution** for his problem.

What is a solution for spilled milk?

_____

_____

villages

Few people live in the small **villages** on the mountain.

What would it be like to visit a small village?

_____

_____

Synonyms

Synonyms are words that have almost the same meaning. *Big* and *large* are synonyms.

🔍 **FIND TEXT EVIDENCE**

I read that Debby "insists that families learn about how solar power can help them" and "They are happy to do what she demands." Insists and demands are synonyms. They both mean "asks for something in a strong way."

Debby believes deeply in her work and insists that families learn about how solar power can help them. They are happy to do what she demands.

Your Turn Think of a synonym for these words in "Lighting Lives."

home, page 3 _____

power, page 4 _____

Alison Wright/Corbis

Ask and Answer Questions

Asking yourself questions helps you think about information in the selection. You can ask yourself questions before, during, and after you read.

Quick Tip

Stop and ask yourself questions about difficult information that you have read or heard. Then reread to find the answers to your questions.

🔍 **FIND TEXT EVIDENCE**

As I read page 4 of "Lighting Lives," I ask myself "What is solar power?" I will reread and look at the photos to find the answer to this question.

Page 4

As she grew, Debby realized she wanted to learn more about solar power. Solar power is electricity that comes from the Sun. Solar panels are put on the roof of a building. The sunlight hits these panels and turns into electricity.

I read that solar power is electricity that comes from the Sun. From this, I understand that solar panels use energy from the Sun.

Your Turn Write a question about how solar power can help people. Reread the parts of the selection that help you to answer it.

_____

_____

Photos and Captions

"Lighting Lives" is narrative nonfiction. It tells a true story about a person by a narrator. It can have text features, such as photos and captions.

Pay close attention to the photos and captions. Authors use photographs and captions to help you understand the key details in a text.

FIND TEXT EVIDENCE

I can use what I read to tell that "Lighting Lives" is narrative nonfiction. A narrator tells about a real person, Debby Tewa.

Page 6

Debby travels **across** lands outside cities in Arizona and New Mexico. She travels to the **countryside**. She helps Hopi and Navajo people get solar power.

Debby believes deeply in her work and **insists** that families learn about how solar power can help them. They are happy to do what she demands. Debby also travels to schools and summer camps to teach Hopi children about solar energy.

Debby helps many Hopi people.

Photos

A photo shows something in the text or gives more information about a topic.

Captions

A caption gives details about a photo.

Your Turn How do the photos and caption on pages 4 and 5 help you understand how solar panels are used?

_____

_____

_____

Author's Purpose

Authors write narrative nonfiction to answer, explain, or describe.

🔍 **FIND TEXT EVIDENCE**

When I read page 4 of "Lighting Lives," I learned how Debby Tewa got the idea to help others. I think this is a clue to the author's purpose.

Clue
Author tells how Debby Tewa got the idea to help people who did not have electricity in their homes.

⬇

Your Turn Continue reading the selection. Fill in a clue and the author's purpose on the graphic organizer.

Clue

Author tells how Debby Tewa got the idea to help people who did not have electricity in their homes.

Clue

Author's Purpose

Respond to Reading

Talk about the prompt below. Think about how the author presents ideas in the text. Use your notes and graphic organizer.

How does the author show how Debby Tewa is "lighting up people's lives"?

_____

_____

_____

_____

_____

_____

_____

Primary and Secondary Sources

People use sources to find information. **Primary sources** come from people's lives. Letters, photographs, and videos may all be primary sources. **Secondary sources** are written by people who studied a topic.

Read the examples of sources below. **Circle** the primary sources. **Underline** secondary sources.

- *Photo of Fourth of July parade from 1976*

- *Encyclopedia entry*

- *Social studies textbook*

- *A speech given by the governor of your state*

History Picture Book Research an important person or event in the history of your town or state. Then create a picture book about your topic with illustrations and captions.

Discuss primary and secondary sources you found in your research.

Quick Tip

In a primary source, a person describes an event that he or she was at or took part in. The person may use *I* or *we* when describing what happened.

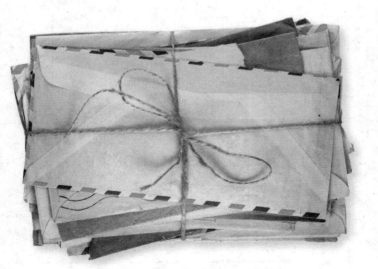

Letters can tell us about important people and events from long ago.

Literature Anthology: pages 212–233

Biblioburro

? **How does the author help you to understand Luis's idea?**

Talk About It Reread page 215. Discuss what Luis pictured in his head as he was thinking.

Text Evidence Complete the chart with details from the illustration and text that show Luis's idea.

Illustration	Text

Write The author helps me understand _____

_____

_____

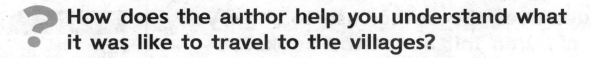

? **How does the author help you understand what it was like to travel to the villages?**

Talk About It Reread pages 220–221. Describe what you see in the illustration.

Cite Text Evidence Write three details you see in the illustration and make an inference about Luis's travels.

I see	I see	I see

Traveling to the villages was...

Write The author helps me understand that _____

_____

_____

Quick Tip

Use these sentence starters to talk about the illustration.

I see...

This makes me think...

Combine Information

Look back at pages 218–219. What words does the author use to describe the villages and hills where Luis traveled every week?

? **What clues does the author use to show you how the children felt about the books?**

Talk About It Reread pages 226–227. Talk about what the children were doing and how they felt.

COLLABORATE

Cite Text Evidence Complete the chart with clues from the text and illustration.

The children were... | The children felt...

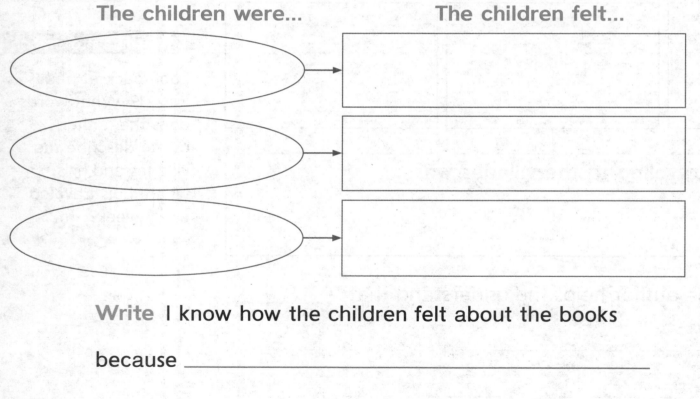

Write I know how the children felt about the books

because _____

_____

_____

Respond to Reading

COLLABORATE

Discuss the prompt below. Review the story and the illustrations for details the author gives about Luis's journey.

How does the author use illustrations to show the difficulty of Luis's journey?

_____

_____

_____

_____

_____

_____

_____

Self-Selected Reading

Choose a text. Read the first two pages. If you don't understand five or more words, choose another text that will let you read for a longer amount of time. Fill in your writer's notebook with the title, author, genre, and your purpose for reading.

Landing on Your Feet

Literature Anthology:
pages 234–237

Before I wake up for school, Dad is already at work. He is an ironworker in the city. Ironworkers build tall buildings and repair giant bridges. They build with heavy metal beams made of iron. When Dad comes home, he likes to cook or do things for our house. He also teaches his favorite sport to kids. Dad is a gymnastics coach at a community center. He teaches girls like me at the same gym where he learned gymnastics as a boy.

Gymnastics is fun but hard to learn. Dad encourages us to practice to get better.

Reread the text. **Underline** details that describe the narrator's dad.

What details help you understand the narrator is a young girl?

_____

_____

_____

_____

COLLABORATE

Discuss why the narrator begins her personal narrative with details about her dad and gymnastics.

(Colored pencils)Tatiana Popova/Shutterstock.com

The ice pack seemed to help Dad relax on the couch. I got pillows so he could put his leg up. Dad said, "I hope my ankle gets better soon. I need to coach the kids on Monday." Now I was really worried. Dad is always there for the kids at the gym. *I have until Monday to help Dad feel better,* I thought.

Reread the text. **Underline** details that show Ryan is concerned about her dad.

Circle details that show Ryan was concerned about the kids at the gym. Why does she have until Monday to help Dad feel better?

_____

_____

_____

Discuss Ryan's feelings and thoughts in the text and why she includes these details.

? **Why did the author write "Landing on Your Feet"?**

COLLABORATE

Talk About It Reread pages 234-237 in the **Literature Anthology**. Discuss the key details in Ryan's story.

Cite Text Evidence Fill in the chart with what Ryan describes took place Friday, over the weekend, and Monday.

Friday	Over the Weekend	Monday

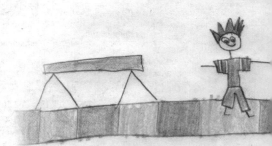

The author wrote her personal narrative _____

_____

_____

Time Words

Ryan uses words and phrases such as "on Monday" and "after practice" to help you understand when each event in her personal narrative story happened.

 FIND TEXT EVIDENCE

Ryan uses the words "one Friday" and "after school" to tell when she was building the toy house. **Circle** words that tell when the next thing in her story happened.

> One Friday, I had free time after school. I was building a toy house for my toy cat. When Dad came home from work, Mom and I knew something was wrong.

Your Turn Reread the first paragraph on page 236. How do you know Dad had hurt his ankle the night before? On what day of the week did this happen?

_____

_____

_____

Quick Tip

Ryan's dad told her about how he had hurt his ankle earlier, or before. Time words will help you to understand when the event had taken place.

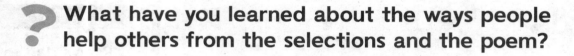

? **What have you learned about the ways people help others from the selections and the poem?**

Talk About It Talk with a partner about how Mouse helps the Lion.

Cite Text Evidence **Circle** clues that show what the author thinks about helping others.

Write The selections I read and this poem help me understand how

_____

_____

_____

_____

_____

_____

_____

Quick Tip

Compare the selections using these sentence starters:

Luis wanted to...

Ryan's dad helped their community by...

The Mouse is able to...

The Mouse and the Lion

A poor thing the Mouse was, and yet

When the Lion got caught in a net,

All his strength was no use

'Twas the poor little Mouse

Who nibbled him out of the net.

SMALL CAUSES MAY PRODUCE GREAT RESULTS

– Walter Crane

Present Your Work

COLLABORATE

With your partner, present your History Picture Book to the class. Use the Presenting Checklist to improve your presentation. Discuss the sentence starters and write your answers.

Our Town

An interesting fact that I learned about the topic is

_____

_____

_____

I would like to know more about _____

_____

_____

Presenting Checklist

☐ Point to the picture as you read each caption.

☐ Speak clearly and tell about the most important information.

☐ Make eye contact with people in the audience.

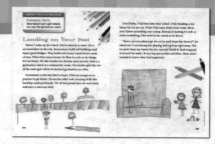

*Literature Anthology:
pages 234-237*

Expert Model

Features of a Personal Narrative

A personal narrative tells a story from the writer's life.

- It is usually written in the first person.

- It has a beginning, middle, and end.

- It uses words and phrases to tell events in order.

Analyze an Expert Model Studying "Landing on Your Feet" will help you learn more about writing a personal narrative. Reread page 235. Answer the questions below.

How does Ryan use dialogue to tell an important detail?

_____

_____

How does Ryan use describing words?

_____

_____

Plan: Brainstorm

Generate Ideas You will write a personal narrative about a time you helped others. Brainstorm words and draw pictures that tell about the times you have helped.

Quick Tip

To help you get started, think about why you helped others and how it made you feel.

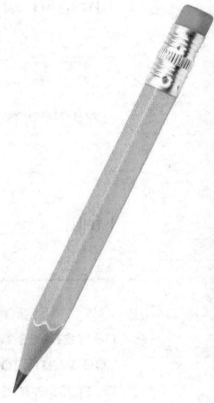

Plan: Choose Your Topic

Writing Prompt Write a personal narrative about doing something good for your school, community, or the environment. You can also write about helping friends or your family. Use your ideas from page 27. Complete these sentences to help you get started.

I helped when I _____

_____

I wanted to do this because _____

_____

I felt _____

_____

Purpose and Audience Authors may write personal narratives to share special experiences. Think about why you want to tell about a time you helped. Explain your purpose for writing in your writer's notebook.

Plan: Organization

Sequence Writers often organize personal narratives with a *beginning, middle,* and *end.* Read the details in the sequence chart. **Circle** words the writer uses to help show when things takes place in the different parts of the story.

Plan In your writer's notebook, make a Sequence chart to organize the details in your personal narrative.

Beginning

One spring day, we decided to repair the playground.

↓

Middle

The next weekend, we had a flea market to raise money for the repairs.

↓

End

By summer, we repaired the playground equipment.

Draft

Focus on an Event The author of "Landing on Your Feet" tells how she helps her dad when he hurts his ankle. Reread this paragraph on page 237. Ryan focuses on taking care of Dad with details about how she helped.

> Over the weekend, Mom and I stayed home with Dad. I got fresh ice packs for his ankle, and I made him lunch and snacks. We watched movies, and I got Dad books to read. Even our kitty, Toast, helped. He lay across Dad to keep him company.

Use the paragraph as a model to write specific details about how you helped. Remember to focus on an event.

_____

_____

_____

Write a Draft Look over your Sequence chart. Use it to help you write your draft in your notebook. Remember to use words and phrases that help your reader understand the sequence of events.

Revise

Conclusion The conclusion of a personal narrative often shares how an author feels about an event. Think about what you want your readers to take away from your writing.

Reread the last paragraph of the selection on page 237. Think about how the author, Ryan, shares how she felt at the end of her story.

Explain how Ryan shows how she felt after helping.

_____

_____

_____

_____

_____

 Revise It's time to revise your draft. Make sure you write a conclusion that tells how you feel about what you did.

Revise: Peer Conferences

Review a Draft Listen carefully as a partner reads his or her work aloud. Begin by telling what you liked about the draft. Make suggestions that you think will make the writing stronger.

Partner Feedback Write one of your partner's suggestions that you will use in the revision of your narrative.

Based on my partner's feedback, I will _____

_____

_____

After you finish giving each other feedback, reflect on the peer conference. What was helpful? What might you do differently next time?

_____

_____

Revision Use the Revising Checklist to help you figure out what text you may need to move, add to, or delete. Remember to use the rubric on page 35 to help you with your revision.

Remember to use the rubric on page 35 to help you with your revision.

Quick Tip

Use these sentence starters to discuss your partner's work.

I enjoyed this part of your draft because...

How about adding more details about...

I have a question about...

✔ **Revising Checklist**

☐ Did I write in the first person and include details?

☐ Does my personal narrative tell about an event?

☐ Did I include a beginning, middle, and end?

☐ Did I write a conclusion?

Edit and Proofread

When you **edit** and **proofread,** you look for and correct mistakes in your writing. Rereading a revised draft several times will help you catch any errors. Use the checklist below to edit your sentences.

Grammar Connections

When you write your personal narrative, make sure you use capital letters for proper nouns. Check for nouns that name specific people, places, or things.

✔ **Editing Checklist**

☐ Do all sentences begin with a capital letter and end with a punctuation mark?

☐ Are present-tense and past-tense forms of action verbs used correctly?

☐ Are all the words spelled correctly?

☐ Are proper nouns capitalized?

List two mistakes you found as you proofread your narrative.

1 _____

_____

2 _____

_____

Publish, Present, and Evaluate

Publishing Create a clean, neat final copy of your personal narrative. You may add illustrations or other visuals to make your published work more interesting.

Presentation Practice your presentation when you are ready to present your work. Use the Presenting Checklist to help you.

Evaluate After you publish and present your personal narrative, use the rubric on the next page to evaluate your writing.

1 What did you do successfully? _____

_____

_____

2 What needs more work? _____

_____

_____

✓ **Presenting Checklist**

☐ Sit up or stand up straight.

☐ Look at the audience.

☐ Read with expression.

☐ Speak loudly so that everyone can hear you.

☐ Answer questions using details from your story.

Listening When you listen actively, you pay close attention to what you hear. When you listen to other students' presentations, take notes to help you better understand their ideas.

What I learned from ....'s presentation:

_____

Questions I have about ....'s presentation:

_____

4	3	2	1
• tells a lively, interesting narrative about being helpful • includes a strong beginning, middle, and end • focuses on one event • uses words accurately to show sequence • has a strong conclusion and tells the author's feelings	• tells a narrative about being helpful • includes a beginning, middle, and end • mostly focuses on one event • uses words to show sequence • has some details about the author's feelings and a conclusion	• tries to tell a narrative about being helpful • attempts to include a beginning, middle, and an end • tries to focus on one event • uses a word or phrase to show sequence • has a detail about the author's feelings but lacks a conclusion	• does not focus on the topic • does not follow a logical sequence of events • does not focus on one event • lacks words that show sequence • does not tell about the author's feelings or have a conclusion

Essential Question

What can we see in the sky?

COLLABORATE Talk about what is happening in the photo. What do you think the girl is looking at?

When you are outside, what do you see in the sky? Talk with a partner about what you can see in the daytime and nighttime skies. Write your ideas in the chart.

Daytime Sky	Nighttime Sky

TAKE NOTES

Use the title and illustrations to write a prediction about what happens in the story.

_____

_____

_____

_____

As you read, make note of:

Interesting Words _____

_____

Key Details _____

_____

_____

_____

Starry Night

Essential Question

?

What can we see in the sky?

Read about what two girls learn when they look at the nighttime sky.

Josie and Ling were good friends. Ling was happy Josie was her **neighbor**. Josie was happy Ling lived nearby, too.

Josie and Ling couldn't wait for the school day to end. They planned a sleepover at Josie's house. They were going to sleep in a tent in Josie's backyard.

As the class was leaving, Mr. Cortes said, "Your weekend homework is to look at the **nighttime** sky and explain what you saw on Monday." The class **grumbled**. "Why the unhappy sounds?" Mr. Cortes asked. "It will be fun looking at the sky at night."

Chris Canga

FIND TEXT EVIDENCE 🔍

Read ▾

Paragraphs 1 and 2
Point of View

Circle pronouns that tell about Josie and Ling.
Underline why they cannot wait for school to end.

Paragraph 3
Reread

Draw a box around the details on the weekend homework. How does the class respond when they get homework?

_____

_____

Reread
Author's Craft

How does the author show Mr. Cortes feels differently from the class about the homework?

FIND TEXT EVIDENCE 🔍

Read

Paragraph 1
Compound Words

Circle the two smaller words in *outdoors*. Why are the girls delighted to be sleeping outdoors?

_____

_____

Paragraph 2
Sequence

Underline text evidence that shows how the girls feel about doing homework at the time.

Reread

Author's Craft

Why is the setting in Josie's backyard at night important to the story?

The girls arrived at Josie's house and were **delighted** to be sleeping outdoors. Josie said, "I'm so happy that we get to sleep in the tent. It will be lots of fun." Then Ling said, "I'll get the sleeping bags and flashlights. I brought flashlights so we can play games in the tent."

Josie's dad poked his head inside the tent. "Girls, it is a good time to do your homework now because it is getting dark," he said. "Awww," they both complained. "Dad," said Josie, "do we have to, now?"

"Yes, I already set up the telescope."

FIND TEXT EVIDENCE 🔍

Read

Paragraph 1

Reread

Why does Josie say, "It's funny that it's called moonlight"? **Circle** details that support your answer.

_____

_____

_____

_____

Fluency

With a partner, practice reading with intonation. Try to raise the tone of your voice when asking a question.

Ling said, "I hope this won't take too long." Josie looked up and spotted a crescent moon. "Did you know the moon's light comes from the sun?" said Josie. "It's funny that it's called **moonlight**." "Yes," said Ling, who was still thinking about playing in the tent.

Josie's dad smiled at the girls and said, "See the stars in the sky? Those points of bright light can form shapes."

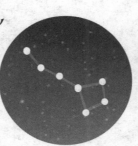

"You can see the Big Dipper," he said. "It's a group of stars that look like a giant spoon in the sky."

The Big Dipper

Chris Canga

FIND TEXT EVIDENCE 🔍

Read

Paragraphs 2-3

Reread

Draw a box around what Ling cries out when she sees a shooting star.

Paragraphs 3-4

Sequence

Underline what Ling says about looking at the stars. How do her feelings change after seeing the shooting star?

_____

_____

_____

Reread

Author's Craft

How does the author use Ling's dialogue to show her excitement?

Josie's dad showed her how to look through the telescope. "Wow, that's more stars than I ever **dreamed** of. I never imagined there could be so many."

It was Ling's turn to look. Ling cried out, "I see a bright light moving in the sky!"

"That's a shooting star!" said Josie's dad.

"This is fun," said Ling. "I really **enjoy** looking at the stars."

Chris Canga

"I think we've seen enough of the nighttime sky," said Josie's dad. "You girls can go play now."

"Aw, Dad, can't we keep looking?" asked Josie. "This is really fun."

"Yes," said Ling. "We have had an **adventure** already, and we haven't even played in the tent yet!"

"You're right, Ling," said Josie. "This has been one exciting night."

Summarize

Was your prediction about the story correct? Use your notes to orally summarize what happens in "Starry Night."

FIND TEXT EVIDENCE

Read

Paragraph 1
Sequence
Circle what Josie's dad says the girls can do now.

Paragraphs 2 and 3
Reread

Underline what Josie asks her dad. What do the girls want to do?

_____

_____

_____

Reread
Author's Craft

How does the author show the girls feel differently about their homework assignment?

Vocabulary

Talk with a partner about each word. Then answer the questions.

adventure

It's an **adventure** to hike in the woods.

What kind of trip would be an adventure?

_____

_____

delighted

Lin is **delighted** to see her grandmother.

What makes you feel delighted?

_____

_____

> **Build Your Word List** Write a sentence using an interesting word you listed on page 38. Use a dictionary to help you.

dreamed

Juan **dreamed** about being an actor.

What is something you dreamed about?

_____

_____

enjoy

We **enjoy** playing in the pool in the summer.

What do you enjoy doing in the summer?

_____

_____

grumbled

My brother **grumbled** because Mom told him to clean his room.

Name something that makes you grumble.

_____

_____

moonlight

The **moonlight** is very bright when the Moon is full.

What can moonlight help you do at night?

_____

_____

neighbor

I went across the street to play with my **neighbor**.

Tell about a neighbor you know.

_____

_____

nighttime

At **nighttime** you can see stars in the sky.

What else can you see at nighttime?

_____

_____

Compound Words

A compound word is made up of two smaller words. The meanings of the smaller words can help you figure out the meaning of a compound word.

FIND TEXT EVIDENCE

I see the word sleepover. *The first part of this word is* sleep, *which means "to close your eyes and rest." The second part of this word is* over, *which can mean "at another place." I think* sleepover *means "sleeping at someone's house."*

They planned a sleepover at Josie's house.

Your Turn Use the smaller words to figure out the meaning of the compound word from page 39.

backyard _____

_____

Chris Canga

Reread

As you read, stop and ask yourself questions about the text. If you can't answer them, reread the parts you do not understand or may have missed. This will help you understand what you read.

Quick Tip

Pay attention to words that tell about actions and words that describe sensory details, such as how something looks or sounds.

🔍 **FIND TEXT EVIDENCE**

On page 41 of "Starry Night," I am not sure what the Big Dipper is. I will reread this part of the story to see if I missed anything.

Page 41

Josie's dad smiled at the girls and said, "See the stars in the sky? Those points of bright light can form shapes."

The Big Dipper

"You can see the Big Dipper," he said. "It's a group of stars that look like a giant spoon in the sky."

When I reread that the Big Dipper is a group of stars that look like a giant spoon in the sky and I look at the picture, I understand what the Big Dipper is.

COLLABORATE
Your Turn What does Ling see when she looks through the telescope? Reread page 42 to answer the question.

Point of View

"Starry Night" is a fiction story with made-up characters and events. A fiction story can be told by a narrator who is not a character in the story. This is called the third-person point of view.

 FIND TEXT EVIDENCE

When I read "Starry Night, I ask myself who is telling the story. Is it a character? Is it someone who is not part of the story?

Readers to Writers

When you read or write fiction, think about who is telling the story. Look for clues, such as the pronouns *he, she,* or *they,* to figure out if the point of view is in third person.

Page 40

The girls arrived at Josie's house and were **delighted** to be sleeping outdoors. Josie said, "I'm so happy that we get to sleep in the tent. It will be lots of fun." Then Ling said, "I'll get the sleeping bags and flashlights. I brought flashlights so we can play games in the tent."

Josie's dad poked his head inside the tent. "Girls, it is a good time to do your homework now because it is getting dark," he said. "Awww," they both complained. "Dad," said Josie, "do we have to, now?"

"Yes, I already set up the telescope."

Point of View

In third-person point of view, the narrator uses words such as *he*, *she*, or *they* to tell the story.

 Your Turn How does the author use third-person point of view to help you understand the characters in the story?

_____

_____

_____

Sequence

The sequence tells the order of events in the story. We can use the words *first, next, then,* and *last* to tell the order of what happens.

 FIND TEXT EVIDENCE

As I read page 39 of "Starry Night," I think about the sequence of the story.

> **First**
> Josie and Ling plan a sleepover.

↓

Your Turn Continue rereading "Starry Night." Fill in the graphic organizer to tell the sequence of events of the story.

> **Quick Tip**
>
> Authors often use signal words and phrases such as *at the beginning, later, before, in the meantime,* and *after* to show the order of events in a story.

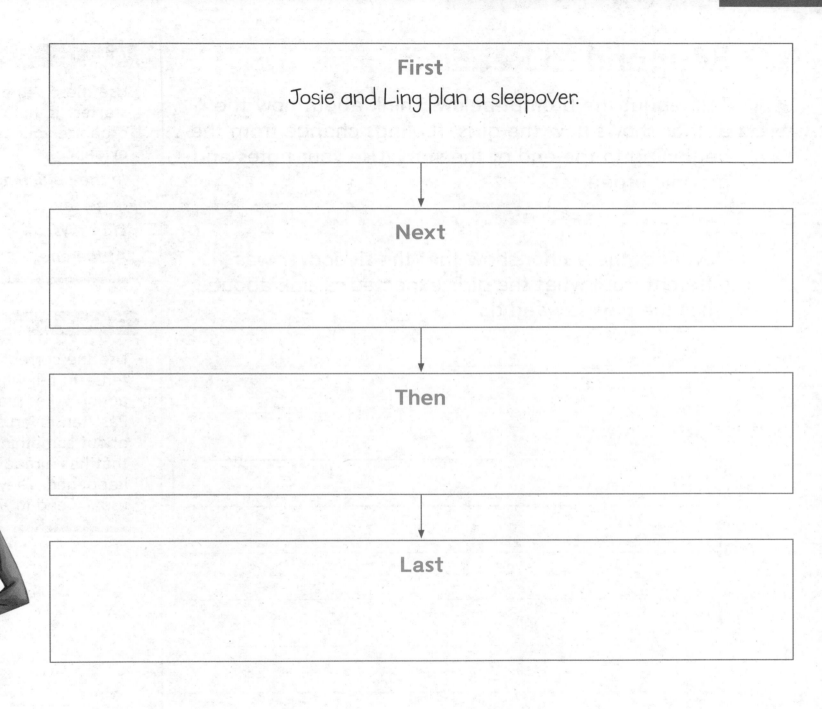

First
Josie and Ling plan a sleepover.

Next

Then

Last

Respond to Reading

COLLABORATE

Talk about the prompt below. Think about how the author shows how the girls' feelings change from the beginning to the end of the story. Use your notes and graphic organizer.

How does the author show that the sleepover was different from what the girls expected? Think about what the girls say and do.

_____

_____

_____

_____

_____

_____

_____

Research Plan

A **research plan** explains how you will find sources and use information. Having a plan is helpful for staying focused on your topic and being organized.

If you wanted to look at the nighttime sky and report on what you saw, how could you organize your plan?

The Night Sky

Moon | The Big Dipper | Shooting Star

Ling and Josie did research about the night sky. This picture shows how they recorded and organized their data. How do you think the drawings and words help them?

COLLABORATE

Moon Phase Report With a partner, make a drawing and write a short report explaining one phase of the Moon. Share your drawing and report with the class.

What source can you use to learn about Moon phases?

_____

How will you remember what the Moon phase looks like and what it is called?

_____

Remember to follow your research plan. Use your notes about sources and the information you get from them.

Literature Anthology: pages 238–256

Mr. Putter & Tabby See the Stars

? **Why does Mrs. Teaberry like to feed Mr. Putter "most of all"?**

Talk About It Reread pages 242 and 243. Talk about how you know that the two characters like each other.

Cite Text Evidence Write clues from the text that tell you Mrs. Teaberry likes Mr. Putter more than other people.

Make Inferences

What do you understand about Mrs. Teaberry and Mr. Putter when they lose track of time while being together?

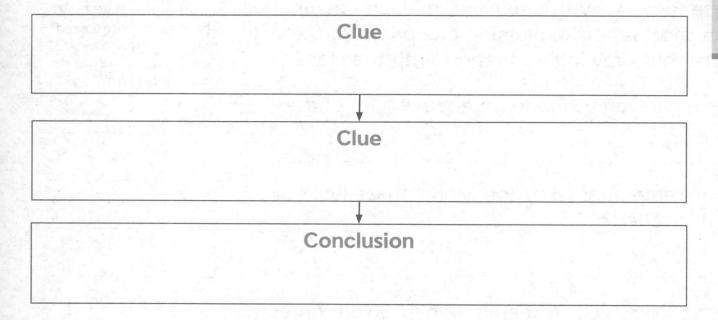

Clue

↓

Clue

↓

Conclusion

Write Mrs. Teaberry likes to feed Mr. Putter the most

because _____

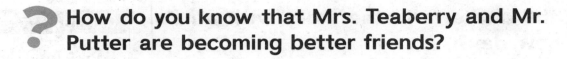

How do you know that Mrs. Teaberry and Mr. Putter are becoming better friends?

Talk About It Reread page 253. Talk about what Mrs. Teaberry and Mr. Putter are doing.

Cite Text Evidence Write clues that tell that Mrs. Teaberry and Mr. Putter are becoming better friends.

Reread page 253.

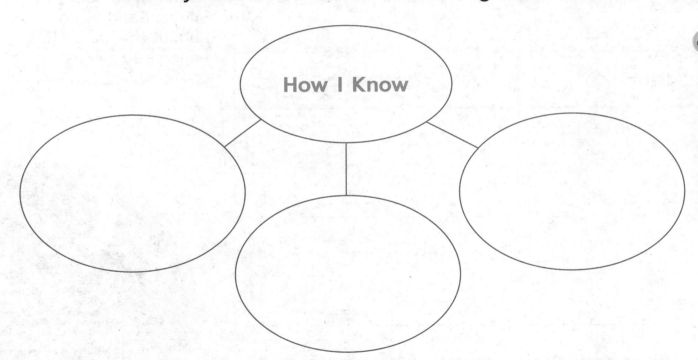

How I Know

Quick Tip

As you read, use these sentence starters to talk about what friends do:

The characters are...
This helps me see...

Combine Information

Use details you already know about Mr. Putter and Mrs. Teaberry to build on your understanding of their friendship.

Write I know that Mrs. Teaberry and Mr. Putter are

becoming better friends because _____

_____

? **Why does the author end the story with a new note on a new day?**

Talk About It Look at the illustration on page 255. Discuss with a partner what Mr. Putter is holding and why.

Cite Text Evidence Write clues that show how the next morning might be the same and how it might be different.

Look at the illustration on page 255.

Same	Different

Write The author ends the story with a new note on a

new day to _____

_____

Quick Tip

Look closely at story illustrations. Sometimes there are details in the pictures that aren't in the text. These details can help you understand more about the characters and story events.

FICTION

Respond to Reading

Discuss the prompt below. Think about everything the author tells you about Mr. Putter and Mrs. Teaberry.

How does the author help you understand the friendship between Mr. Putter and Mrs. Teaberry?

Quick Tip

Use these sentence frames to organize your text evidence.

The author says that Mr. Putter...

The author says that Mrs. Teaberry...

This shows...

Self-Selected Reading

Choose a text. In your writer's notebook, write the title, author, and genre of the book. As you read, make a connection to ideas in other texts you read or to a personal experience. Write your ideas in your writer's notebook.

Day to Night

Your alarm clock rings. *Beep! Beep! Beep!* You turn it off, stretch, and get out of bed. You look out the window and see the daytime sky.

The Daytime Sky

The sky is light today. It is blue with white clouds and the bright Sun. The Sun is the brightest object in the sky. It looks small, but that is because it is far from Earth.

Sometimes the daytime sky has clouds.

Marc Romanelli/Stone/Getty Images

Literature Anthology: pages 258-261

Reread paragraph 1. How does the author grab your attention at the beginning? **Draw a box** around the evidence. Why does the author start the selection that way?

_____

_____

_____

Reread paragraph 2. **Underline** a sentence that tells what the daytime sky looks like.

COLLABORATE

Circle the title. Talk with a partner about whether it is a good one. Then choose a new title for the selection together.

The Nighttime Sky

At the end of the day, you look out the window before you get into bed. The sky is dark. It is nighttime. Tonight you see part of the Moon. Without the bright light from the Sun, you are able to see light from many stars.

The stars look like tiny points of light, but each one is very big.

Reread the paragraph. **Underline** details about the two major differences between the daytime sky and the nighttime sky. Write them here.

_____

_____

_____

COLLABORATE

Talk about what you learn about the night sky from the photograph.

Why did the author write "Day to Night"?

Talk About It Reread pages 258-261. Talk with a partner about what you learned from "Day to Night."

Cite Text Evidence Write facts you learned from the text, then write why the author wrote "Day to Night."

Quick Tip

"Day to Night" is an expository text. Authors write expository texts to inform readers. To figure out what an author is trying to inform you about, ask yourself "What does the author want me to learn?"

Fact	Fact	Fact

The author wrote this to...

Write The author wrote "Day to Night" to _____

_____

_____

_____

Heads

Expository texts often have heads that separate the text into parts. The heads are usually printed in big, bold type. Authors use them to tell you what the different sections of the text are about.

FIND TEXT EVIDENCE

Take another look at "Day to Night." Write the section heads on the lines below.

_____   _____

_____   _____

_____

Your Turn Look at the heads in "Day to Night" one more time. Why do you think some are orange and some are blue?

_____

_____

_____

Quick Tip

Heads tell you what to expect in a section. Sometimes they give you a clue about the section's most important ideas. When you go back to find information, looking at heads and subheads can help you find it quickly.

How do the selections you read and the painting help you understand how the sky changes from day to night?

Talk About It Talk about what you see in the sky in the painting. Talk about what people see in the sky as it changes from day to night.

Cite Text Evidence **Circle** a clue in the caption that tells you what time of day it is in the painting.

Write The selections and the painting show

_____

_____

_____

_____

_____

_____

_____

Quick Tip

Describe the evening sky using these sentence starters:

Between day and night, I can see…

Without the bright light from the Sun, I can see…

This painting of an evening sky by William Turner shows daylight fading on the horizon and a comet in the sky.

Present Your Work

With your partner, plan how you will present your Moon phase report and drawing to the class. Discuss the sentence starters below and write your answers.

> **First Quarter Moon**
>
> Moon Phase:
> First Quarter
>
> Comes a week after the new moon.
>
> Rises at noon and sets around midnight.

Our favorite Moon phase is _____

_____

because_____

_____

Talk About It

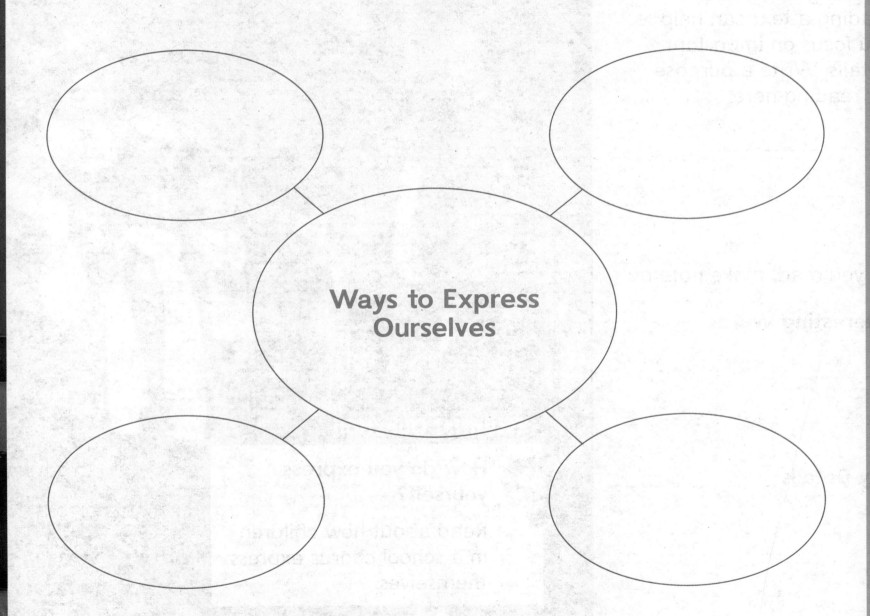

People express themselves in many ways to show their feelings and share their thoughts. Talk about how the boys in the photo are expressing themselves. How do you like to express yourself? Write your ideas in the web.

Ways to Express Ourselves

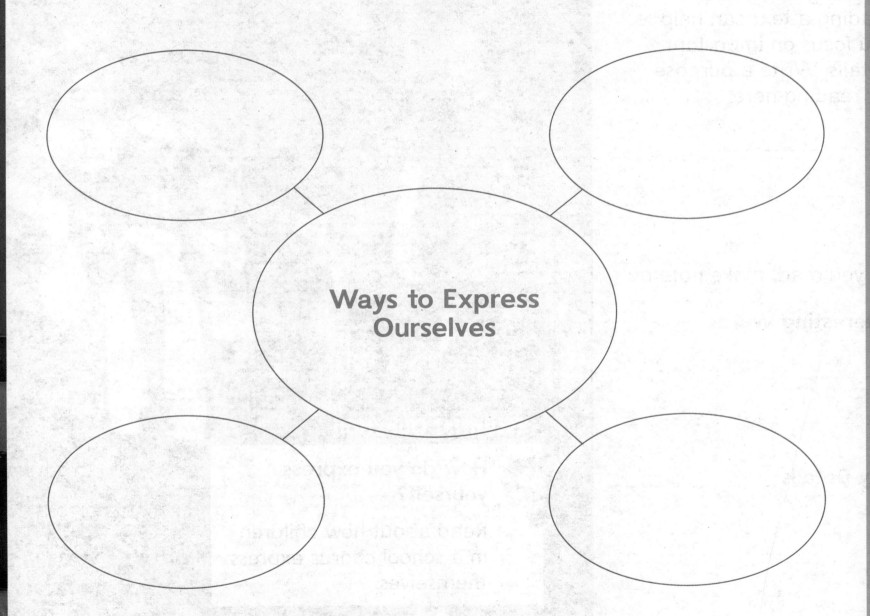

TAKE NOTES

Knowing why you are reading a text can help you focus on important details. Write a purpose for reading here.

_____

_____

_____

As you read, make note of:

Interesting Words _____

_____

_____

Key Details _____

_____

_____

Essential Question

How do you express yourself?

Read about how children in a school chorus express themselves.

They've Got the Beat!

Some students in New York really sing their hearts out! That's because they are in the school chorus at Public School 22.

These students from Staten Island had a **concert** at the White House. They sang at a Hollywood awards show. Audiences have clapped and **cheered** them on. These kids are always asked to return.

How does it feel to sing on stage? "I get nervous singing for a big audience," Brianna Crispino recalls. "But when I see the joy on their faces, I get excited."

Brianna Crispino,
Public School 22 Chorus Member

FIND TEXT EVIDENCE 🔍

Read

Paragraphs 1-2
Main Idea and Key Details
Circle words that describe where the chorus is from. **Draw a box** around places where they traveled to sing.

Paragraph 3
Ask and Answer Questions
Think of a question about the feelings Brianna describes. Write it here.

_____

_____

Underline clues that help answer your question.

Reread

Author's Craft

How does the author grab your attention in the opening paragraph?

Sounds Good

Read

Paragraph 1

Main Idea and Key Details

Underline the definitions of the two groups of singers. Why do all the singers keep the rhythm?

_____

_____

Paragraph 2 and Graph
Bar Graphs

In the bar graph, **circle** the type of voice with the fewest singers.

Reread

Author's Craft

How does the author compare the P.S. 22 chorus with most adult choruses?

The P.S.22 chorus is divided into two groups. The sopranos sing high notes. The altos sing lower **sounds**. **Instruments** like drums sometimes keep the beat. It's important to keep the **rhythm** so they make the right sounds together.

Most adult choruses have four groups of voices. Here's a look at the number of each type of voice in one adult chorus from Pennsylvania.

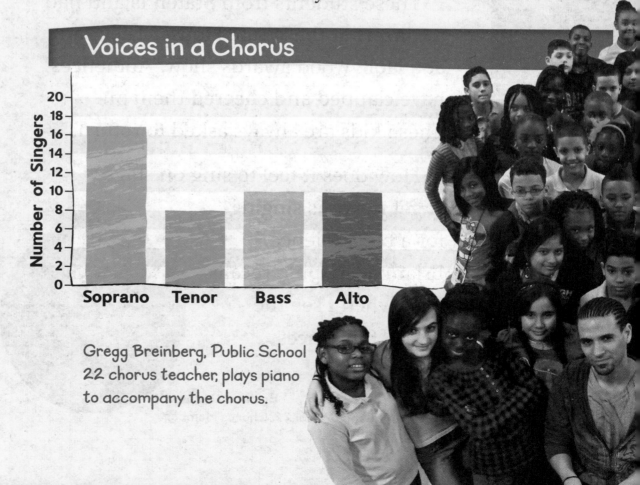

Voices in a Chorus

Bar graph — Number of Singers (y-axis, 0–20): Soprano 17, Tenor 8, Bass 10, Alto 10

Gregg Breinberg, Public School 22 chorus teacher, plays piano to accompany the chorus.

Bebeto Matthews/AP Images

Musical Expression

Being part of the chorus is hard work. The chorus members won't disagree. They practice for three hours each week.

Gregg Breinberg, their teacher, encourages the chorus to use **movements**. They move their hands to show how the songs make them feel. "They have their own movements because nobody feels **music** the same way," he explains.

The chorus members **understand** that singing in a chorus is a big job. "We just want to give it our best!" one student says.

Summarize

Use your notes to orally summarize the key details in "They've Got the Beat!"

TEXT EVIDENCE

FIND TEXT EVIDENCE

Read

Paragraph 1
Prefixes
The prefix *dis-* means "opposite of." **Circle** the word with the prefix *dis-*. Write the word's meaning.

_____

_____

Paragraph 2
Ask and Answer Questions
Why does Gregg Breinberg encourage the chorus to use movements? **Underline** text evidence to answer.

Reread
Author's Craft

How does the author use a student's comment to support ideas in the text?

Vocabulary

**Talk with a partner about each word.
Then answer the questions.**

cheered

We **cheered** for the runners in the race.

Who have you cheered for?

_____

_____

concert

Jack played the drums in the **concert**.

Tell about a concert you saw.

_____

_____

> **Build Your Word List** Choose an interesting word that you noted while reading. Look up its meaning in the dictionary. Write a sentence using the word in your notebook.

instrument

A violin is a musical **instrument**.

What musical instruments can you name?

_____

_____

_____

movements

The dancer's **movements** are exciting.

What movements do you make when you dance?

_____

_____

_____

music

Dad's favorite kind of **music** is jazz.

What is your favorite kind of music?

_____

_____

rhythm

We clapped to the **rhythm** of the song.

What is another word for rhythm?

_____

_____

sounds

A flute can make soft **sounds**.

What can make really loud sounds?

_____

_____

understand

Ken did not **understand** the rules of the game.

What can you do when a paragraph is hard to understand?

_____

_____

Prefixes

A prefix is a word part at the beginning of a word. You can separate the root word from a prefix such as *re-* or *dis-* to figure out a word's meaning.

🔍 **FIND TEXT EVIDENCE**

I'm not sure what return *means. I know* turn *means "to move around in a circle." The prefix* re- *means "again" or "back."* Return *means "to come around again."*

These kids are always asked to return .

Your Turn Use the prefix *re-* to help you understand a word from the selection. Write the definition. Then use the word in a sentence in your writer's notebook.

recalls, page 65 _____

_____

Ask and Answer Questions

When you read, asking questions helps you think about key details of the text that you may have missed or do not understand.

FIND TEXT EVIDENCE

As I read page 67 of "They've Got the Beat," I ask myself, "Why is singing in the chorus hard work?" I will reread to find the answer.

Page 67

Being part of the chorus is hard work. The chorus members won't disagree. They practice for three hours each week.

I reread that the chorus practices "three hours each week." This text evidence answers my question.

Your Turn Think of a question you have about the selection. Reread parts of the text to help you answer the question. Write your question and answer here.

_____

_____

Bar Graphs

"They've Got the Beat!" is an expository text. It gives facts and information about a topic. It has text features, such as a graph, photographs, and headings.

Quick Tip

Look at the numbers on the left of the graph to find out the exact size of each group of singers.

🔍 FIND TEXT EVIDENCE

I know that "They've Got the Beat" is an expository text. It gives information about real students. It has a graph with information about a chorus.

Page 66

Sounds Good

The P.S.22 chorus is divided into two groups. The sopranos sing high notes. The altos sing lower **sounds**. **Instruments** like drums sometimes keep the beat. It's important to keep the **rhythm** so they make the right sounds together.

Most adult choruses have four groups of voices. Here's a look at the number of each type of voice in one adult chorus from Pennsylvania.

Voices in a Chorus

Number of Singers — Soprano, Tenor, Bass, Alto

Gregg Breinberg, Public School 22 chorus teacher, plays piano to accompany the chorus.

Bar Graphs

A bar graph uses bars to show and compare information.

Your Turn What did you learn from information in the graph?

COLLABORATE

_____

_____

_____

Main Idea and Key Details

Quick Tip

Think about what the key details have in common, or what they all tell about. This will help you to identify the main idea.

The main idea is the most important point an author makes about a topic. Key details tell about and support the main idea.

 FIND TEXT EVIDENCE

As I read page 65 of "They've Got the Beat," I understand a key detail about this chorus is that they have performed at special places like the White House.

Detail

They performed at the White House.

 Your Turn Continue rereading the selection. List the key details and the main idea in the graphic organizer.

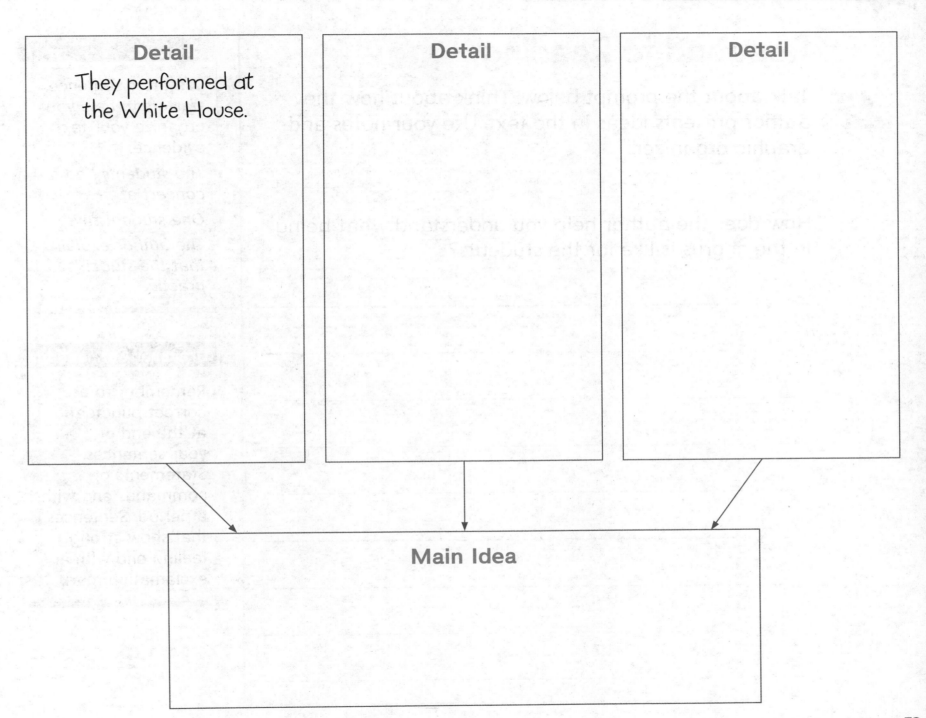

Detail

They performed at the White House.

Detail

Detail

Main Idea

Respond to Reading

COLLABORATE

Talk about the prompt below. Think about how the author presents ideas in the text. Use your notes and graphic organizer.

How does the author help you understand what being in the chorus is like for the students?

_____

_____

_____

_____

_____

_____

_____

Quick Tip

Use these sentence starters to help you organize your text evidence.

The students had a concert at...

One student says...

The author explains that the students practice...

Grammar Connections

Remember to use correct punctuation at the end of your sentences. Statements or commands end with a period. Sentences that show strong feeling end with an exclamation mark.

Relevant Information

Quick Tip

Remember to paraphrase relevant information by taking notes in your own words. Do not take notes on information you already know. You may note other interesting facts about a topic if you think the information could be helpful.

Relevant information is facts and details that tell about a topic. To identify relevant information, make sure the fact or detail answers one of your research questions.

Read the paragraph. Circle relevant information that answers the question: *Why is the song patriotic?*

> Everyone knows the song "Yankee Doodle." Colonial soldiers sang it with pride during the American Revolution. It was actually written by someone in the British army. Kids in the U.S. still sing it today.

Patriotic Song Collage With a partner, choose a patriotic song such "America the Beautiful." Take notes on relevant information that answers your questions about the song. Label the collage and write sentences about the song using your notes.

The name of the patriotic song I will research is

_____

_____

SerrNovik/iStock/Getty Images

Literature Anthology:
pages 262–265

Many Ways to Enjoy Music

? **How does the author help you sense the excitement of a concert?**

Talk About It Reread page 263. Discuss details that describe what may happen at a concert.

Text Evidence What words are used to describe the concert? Write the text evidence in the web.

 Make Inferences

Remember that an inference is your best guess from the text evidence. Why does the author want you to sense the excitement of a concert?

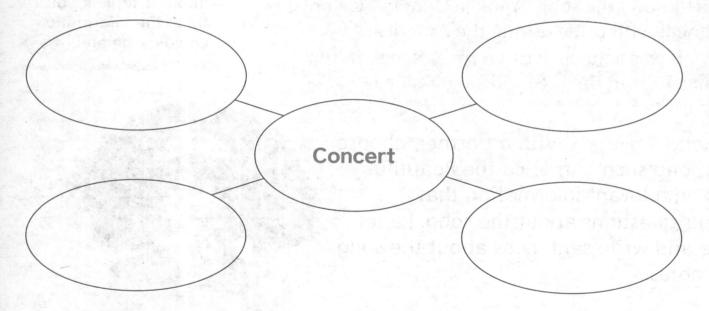

Concert

Write The author helps me sense the excitement of the

concert _____

_____

? **Why does the author describe watching an interpreter and using technology?**

Talk About It Look back at pages 264–265. Discuss the details about interpreters and the technology of a special chair.

Cite Text Evidence What details help you understand how music can be enjoyed in different ways? Write text evidence in the chart.

Interpreter	Special Chair

Write The author wants readers to understand how _____

_____

_____

Respond to Reading

Discuss the prompt below. Think about the main idea and the key details in the selection as you respond.

Why is "Many Ways to Enjoy Music" a good title for this selection?

_____

_____

_____

_____

_____

_____

_____

_____

Self-Selected Reading

Choose a text. In your writer's notebook, write the title, author, and genre of the book. As you read, make a connection to ideas in other texts you read, or a personal experience. Write your ideas in your writer's notebook.

A Musical Museum

Humans can hear almost every sound in nature. But some animals hear sounds you can't hear. Dogs and bats, for example, can hear very high sounds that don't reach human ears. What sounds do you like to listen to?

Sound is the energy things make when they move back and forth. Those back and forth movements are called vibrations.

Energy You Hear

Ears hear vibrations as sound

Sound vibrations move through air

Source of sound vibrations

Literature Anthology: pages 266–267

Reread the text. **Underline** what humans can hear. **Draw a box** around the definition of sound.

Look back at the diagram. How do our ears hear vibrations?

_____

_____

COLLABORATE

Discuss how the diagram shows how a person can hear a drum.

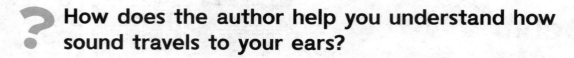
? **How does the author help you understand how sound travels to your ears?**

Talk About It Reread page 267 in the **Literature Anthology.** Discuss details that explain what sound is.

Cite Text Evidence Complete the chart. Write text evidence that explains how people hear sound.

"Back and forth movements are called vibrations."

↓

↓

↓

Write The author explains _____

_____

_____

> ### Quick Tip
>
> In "A Musical Museum," the author explains how sound is created and travels to your ears. Pay attention to how each detail is connected. This will make the text easier to understand.

Diagrams

A diagram is a graphic feature used in expository texts. Authors use diagrams to show the special parts of something or to explain how something works.

FIND TEXT EVIDENCE

Look back at the diagram on page 267. What three steps are shown in the diagram?

1. _____

2. _____

3. _____

Your Turn Reread the second paragraph. Discuss the information from the text shown in the diagram. What is an example of a text detail the author did not include in the diagram?

_____

_____

_____

Readers to Writers

Label each step in a diagram with a simple sentence or a phrase. Include only the most important information. You may number each step to show sequence, or the correct order of the information.

MAKE CONNECTIONS

? **What have you learned from the selections and the Japanese print about expressing yourself through music?**

Talk About It Look at the print and read the caption. Talk with a partner about what the people are doing.

Cite Text Evidence **Underline** text evidence in the caption that tells what the artist shows. **Circle** instruments in the picture that some of the women are playing.

Write From the selections and the Japanese print, I have learned that expressing yourself through music can mean

_____

_____

_____

_____

_____

_____

Quick Tip

A personal connection is relating details you have read, heard, or seen to your own life. Think about how you can describe a personal connection you have to music.

This Japanese print, called an Ukiyo-e, shows a gathering of women playing a variety of musical instruments.

Intonation

Read aloud at a rate, or speed, that is easy for your listeners to understand. Change the tone of your voice to express meaning to listeners. Stress important words or phrases by reading them slowly. Pause for a comma or period, and raise your voice at the end of a question.

Page 65

Some students in New York really sing their hearts out! That's because they are in the school chorus at Public School 22.

I see an exclamation point. I can read loudly to show excitement. I can stress important words, such as "the school chorus."

Your Turn Turn back to page 65. Take turns reading paragraphs from "They've Got the Beat" with a partner. Pay attention to your intonation so that the author's ideas are easy to understand. Afterward, think about how you did. Complete these sentences.

I remembered to _____

Next time I will _____

Carrie Devorah/WENN.com/Newscom

Expert Model

Literature Anthology: pages 262–265

Features of Expository Essay

Authors write expository essays to give information about a topic.

- Expository essays give facts and information.
- It can have text features such as photos and captions.
- It has a strong opening and a conclusion.

Word Wise

The author uses phrases, such as *one way* and *another way* to help you understand that there are different ways to enjoy music.

Analyze an Expert Model Studying "Many Ways to Enjoy Music" will help you learn to write an expository essay. Reread page 265. Answer the questions below.

COLLABORATE

How does the author use language to help you understand how the special chair works?

_____

_____

What is the author's concluding statement?

_____

_____

Plan: Brainstorm

Generate Ideas You will write an expository essay that tells about music or a musical instrument. To begin, brainstorm types of music and words related to music. Draw pictures of musical instruments. You will choose your topic from your ideas.

Quick Tip

To help you get started, think about a favorite musical instrument or a type of music you want to learn more about. You may also look through books, magazines, or websites to find pictures and words related to music.

Stockbyte/SuperStock

Plan: Choose Your Topic

Writing Prompt Write an expository essay that tells about a type of music or a musical instrument. Go back to the ideas you brainstormed on page 85 to choose your topic. Complete these sentences to help you get started.

My topic is _____

_____

This topic interests me because _____

_____

_____

Go back to the ideas you brainstormed on page 85 to choose your topic.

Purpose and Audience Authors write expository essays to teach readers about an interesting topic. They may explain or describe information to answer questions. Think about why you chose your topic. Then write your purpose for writing in your writer's notebook.

jianying yin/Getty Images

Plan: Research

Choose and Evaluate Sources Reliable sources have facts that can be proven to be correct. To evaluate sources of information you can use, make sure that:

- the author is an expert on your topic.
- the information is accurate and not too difficult.

 Mark these types of sources as reliable or not reliable.

Quick Tip

Remember to write source information so you can cite the sources you used. Write the author, title, website or publisher, date, and page numbers.

Sources	Reliable	Not Reliable
textbooks	✓	
blogs or social media		
encyclopedias		
education websites		

 Plan In your writer's notebook, list two sources that you can use to research your topic.

Draft

Paragraphs A paragraph is a group of sentences that tell about one idea. The first word of a paragraph is usually indented. Reread page 264 of "Many Ways to Enjoy Music" in the **Literature Anthology**.

What idea do the details in the paragraph tell about?

_____

Now use the paragraph as a model to write a paragraph of your essay. Make sure the details tell about one idea.

_____

_____

_____

 Write a Draft Use the information you gathered from your sources to write a draft in your writer's notebook.

┌─ **Digital Tools** ──────────────────────────────
To learn more about creating an outline, watch "Outline to Draft." Go to **my.mheducation.com**.
└──

> **Quick Tip**
>
> Outline paragraphs for your essay. Write a sentence that tells what a paragraph will be about. Under the sentence, list details from your notes that tell about the idea.

Revise

Strong Opening A strong opening will grab the reader's attention so that he or she wants to read more. A strong opening also states the topic of the expository essay.

Reread a student's opening paragraph below. Talk with a partner about how it grabs your attention. Write your ideas on the lines below.

> What is better than banging on the drums in the middle of a school day? Nothing, in my opinion. Music class is my favorite part of the day. We learn about instruments and make music.

_____

_____

_____

Revise It's time to revise your draft. Think about how you can write a strong opening to your essay. Make sure each paragraph has facts that tell about one idea.

©KidStock/Blend Images LLC

Revise: Peer Conferences

Review a Draft Listen carefully as a partner reads his or her work aloud. Begin by telling what you like about the draft. Make suggestions that you think will make the writing stronger.

Partner Feedback Write one of your partner's suggestions that you will use in the revision of your text.

Based on my partner's feedback, I will _____

_____

_____

After you finish giving each other feedback, reflect on the peer conference. What was helpful? What might you do differently next time?

_____

_____

Revision Use the Revising Checklist to help you figure out what text you may need to move, add to, or delete. Remember to use the rubric on page 93 to help you with your revision.

Remember to use the rubric on page 93 to help you with your revision.

Quick Tip

Use these sentence starters to discuss your partner's work.

Where did you find the information about...

Can you explain how...

I think that it would be clearer to say...

✔ Revising Checklist

☐ Does my essay tell about the topic?

☐ Does each paragraph tell about one idea?

☐ Does it have a strong opening?

☐ Does it have a conclusion?

☐ Are the sources clearly cited?

Edit and Proofread

When you **edit** and **proofread**, you look for and correct mistakes in your writing. Rereading a revised draft several times will help you catch any errors. Use the checklist below to edit your sentences.

✔ Editing Checklist

- ☐ Do all sentences end with the correct punctuation mark?
- ☐ Does the verb agree with the subject in each sentence?
- ☐ Are the verbs used correctly in the past and future tenses?
- ☐ Is the word "have" used correctly?
- ☐ Are all of the words spelled correctly?

List two mistakes you found as you proofread your text.

1 _____

_____

2 _____

_____

Publish, Present, and Evaluate

Publishing Create a neat, clean final copy of your expository essay. Add illustrations or a diagram to make your published work more interesting.

Presentation Practice your presentation when you are ready to present your work. Use the Presenting Checklist to help you.

Evaluate After you publish and present your essay, use the rubric on the next page to evaluate your writing.

1 What did you do successfully? _____

_____

_____

2 What needs more work? _____

_____

_____

✓ Presenting Checklist

- ☐ Sit up or stand up straight.
- ☐ Look at different people in the audience.
- ☐ Speak slowly and clearly.
- ☐ Speak loudly so that everyone can hear you.
- ☐ Answer questions using facts from your text.

Listening When you listen actively, you pay close attention to what you hear. When you listen to other students' presentations, take notes to help you better understand their ideas.

What I learned from ....'s presentation:

_____

Questions I have about ....'s presentation:

_____

4	3	2	1
• focuses on a topic related to music	• focuses mostly on one topic related to music	• lacks focus on a topic	• does not focus on a topic
• has a strong opening and a concluding statement or section	• introduces the topic in the opening and has a conclusion	• does not have a strong opening and lacks a conclusion	• does not have an opening or a conclusion
• each paragraph tells about an idea	• in each paragraph, most details relate to one idea	• attempts to write complete paragraphs	• does not organize ideas into paragraphs
• is free or almost free of errors	• has few errors	• has errors that distract from the meaning of the essay	• has many errors that make the essay hard to understand

⊙ Spiral Review

You have learned new skills and strategies in Unit 3 that will help you to read and understand texts. Now it is time to practice what you have learned.

- **Compound Words**
- **Prefixes**
- **Author's Purpose**
- **Sequence**
- **Main Idea and Key Details**
- **Photos and Captions**
- **Point of View**

Connect to Content

- **Personal Narrative**
- **Respond to the Read Aloud**
- **Community Helpers Ad**

Read the selection and choose the best answer to each question.

Landing the Eagle

[1]　Astronaut Neil Armstrong was sitting in a tiny spaceship called *Eagle*. He was flying toward the Moon. Neil watched as *Eagle* got closer to the Moon. Suddenly, he saw a big problem ahead. *Eagle's* landing computers were heading toward a field of giant rocks the size of cars! He knew that this landing spot was <u>unsafe</u>. The rocks could tip over *Eagle*. That would damage his ship. He would be unable to leave the Moon forever!

[2]　Neil made a decision. He turned off the computers. He would steer the ship himself. He was worried about landing the ship safely. The ship was also almost out of fuel. Neil had to find a place to land soon!

3   Neil guided *Eagle* carefully past the giant rocks. He saw a wide, flat field up ahead.

4   "That is the place!" he thought. Slowly, he lowered *Eagle* onto the field. But his rocket boosters blew a big cloud of dust into the air. Neil was blinded as he guided *Eagle* down.

5   Finally, *Eagle's* small feet thumped onto the Moon. Neil breathed a sigh of relief. He clicked his radio and sent a happy message back home. "Houston . . . The Eagle has landed."

Neil Armstrong was the first person to walk on the Moon. He placed a flag on the Moon to show that America's astronauts reached it first.

National Aeronautics and Space Administration (NASA)

SHOW WHAT YOU LEARNED

1 In paragraph 1, the reader can use the prefix "un-" to know that the word <u>unsafe</u> means —

A Very safe

B Not safe

C Somewhat safe

D Able to be safe

Quick Tip

You can separate the root word from a prefix, such as *re-* or *un-*, to help you figure out what the word means.

2 Which sentence from the article best helps the reader understand that *Eagle* is fragile?

F *The rocks could tip over* Eagle.

G *He would be unable to leave the Moon forever!*

H *But his rocket boosters blew a big cloud of dust into the air.*

J *"Houston . . . The Eagle has landed."*

3 Which idea from the article is supported by the photograph?

A Neil Armstrong did great things for space travel.

B *Eagle* is difficult to fly for an astronaut.

C Neil Armstrong was worried about landing on the Moon.

D *Eagle* is small and can be broken easily.

4 The author wrote the article most likely to —

F convince the reader to become an astronaut

G share information about an interesting space program

H tell the reader about an important person in history

J explain how to land a spaceship on the Moon

Read the selection and choose the best answer to each question.

A Shower in the Sky

1.   The sky grew dark. Rico was excited. Tonight was going to be the best meteor shower of the year. Rico had looked forward to this night for a long time. He and his father drove to the top of a dark hill. They lay two sleeping bags on a tarp in the grass. Then they watched the dark sky.

2.   Suddenly Rico saw a bright streak in the sky. A meteor! It lasted less than a second. Then it was gone.

3.   "I saw one!" he shouted.

4   Rico's father saw another and pointed. A meteor streaked out across the sky!

5   Rico and his father counted each meteor. At first, they saw a meteor every one or two seconds.

6   Then the meteors started coming more slowly. Sometimes one minute would pass before they saw another. Then two minutes. More time passed. Rico counted ten minutes before another meteor shot across the sky.

7   "The shower is almost over," his father said. "You can close your eyes now and sleep."

8   Rico wanted to watch the starry sky all night long. But his sleeping bag was cozy. He closed his eyes. Rico pictured meteors dancing across his <u>eyelids</u> as he drifted off to sleep.

1. Which detail belongs in the empty box in the chart?

    A Rico looks forward to the meteor shower.

    B Rico and his father lay out sleeping bags.

    C Rico and his father count each meteor.

    D Rico drifts off to sleep.

2. How do you know that the story is told in the third person point of view?

    F The narrator is a character in the story.

    G The narrator is quoted in the story.

    H The narrator plays a big role in helping Rico and his father look at the sky.

    J The narrator tells what the characters are doing but is not in the story.

3. Which words in paragraph 8 help you understand the meaning of <u>eyelids</u>?

    A *watch the starry sky*

    B *all night long*

    C *closed his eyes*

    D *meteors dancing*

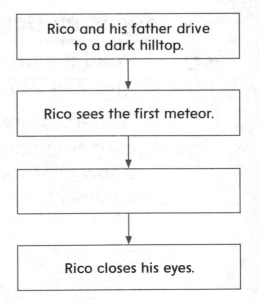

Rico and his father drive to a dark hilltop.

↓

Rico sees the first meteor.

↓

↓

Rico closes his eyes.

Quick Tip

The third person point of view happens when a narrator tells a story about events that happened.

Focus on Genre

Reread the personal narrative "Landing on Your Feet" on pages 234-237.

- When you read the story, how can you tell it is a personal narrative? What words does the author use to show that the story is written in the first person point of view?

- What are the parts of the story that make you think it could really take place in the real world?

Talk about how the author uses time-order words to tell events in order. Then use the Graphic Organizer to write down the parts of the story that happen in the beginning, middle, and end of the story.

> ### Quick Tip
> The first person point of view happens when someone tells their own story. A personal narrative is usually written in the first person.

Beginning

One Friday, _____

Middle

Over the weekend, _____

End

On Monday, _____

Prefixes

COLLABORATE

A prefix is a word part at the beginning of a word. You can separate a prefix, such as *un-* or *dis-,* from the root word. If you know the meaning of a prefix, it can help you figure out the meaning of many words.

Examples of prefixes and their meanings:

dis-	not	disagree
re-	again	return
un-	not	unfair

Read the words below. Write the meaning of each word. Use the chart above to help.

dislike _____

replay _____

unhappy _____

disappear _____

relearn _____

Write a Personal Narrative

COLLABORATE

Write a personal narrative about a musical performance. It could be about a time when you gave your own performance or when you listened to a performance. Here are some tips:

- Your writing should be a true story.

- Include details about how the event made you feel.

- Make sure your story has a beginning, middle, and end.

- Use time-order words like *first, next,* and *finally* to help your reader know what order the events happened.

- Use the lines below to help you get started.

Story Title: _____

Setting: _____

Beginning: _____

Middle: _____

End: _____

Respond to the Read Aloud

The main events tell about what happens in the story in the beginning, middle, and end. The events help you to understand the order of the story, the characters, and the plot.

Listen to "The Hidden Sun."

Describe what happens in the story.

Write about three of the main events.

Event
Event
Event

Community Helpers Ad

A community helper is someone who helps other people. Community helpers may work at animal shelters or libraries. They may fight fires or drive ambulances. Many places use community helpers to get things done.

Choose a helper in your community. Imagine that you are looking for volunteers to join your community helper. Write an advertisement to tell people what they will do and how they will help. You can use print or online resources to find information for your ad.

Write the name or job of the community helper you will write about.

_____

What is one thing your community helper does?

_____

Write your ideas on what your ad will look like below.

_____

_____

Quick Tip

An ad has a slogan and instructions about how to get involved. It usually includes information, such as a website where you can learn more about the subject.

TRACK YOUR PROGRESS

What Did You Learn?

Use the rubric to evaluate yourself on the skills that you learned in this unit. Circle your scores below.

	excellent	good	fair	needs work
Compound Words	4	3	2	1
Prefixes	4	3	2	1
Author's Purpose	4	3	2	1
Sequence	4	3	2	1
Main Idea and Key Details	4	3	2	1
Photos and Captions	4	3	2	1
Point of View	4	3	2	1

What is something you want to get better at?

_____

Text to Self Think about the texts you read in this unit. Tell your partner about a personal connection you made to one of the texts. Use the sentence starter to help you.

I made a connection to . . . because . . .

Present Your Work

COLLABORATE

With your partner, plan how you will present your collage to the class. Use the Presenting Checklist to help you. Discuss the sentence starters below and write your answers.

The song makes me feel _____

_____

_____

_____

I would like to know more about _____

_____

_____

_____

Quick Tip

Decide which information each of you will share. Practice together before you present to the class.

✓ **Presenting Checklist**

☐ Practice with your partner in front of a friend.

☐ Point to each part of your collage as you talk about it.

☐ Stand up straight and make eye contact with your audience.

☐ Speak clearly and slowly so the class can understand you.